THE ANCESTRAL FEAR HYPOTHESIS

The Ancestral Fear Hypothesis

DAKOTA FRANDSEN

First Printing, 2025

Contents

Abstract

This research report explores a speculative but scientifically-grounded hypothesis: that the uncanny valley phenomenon—the visceral discomfort humans experience when confronted with almost-human entities—may represent an inherited fear response originating from ancient encounters between Homo sapiens and Neanderthals. By synthesizing evidence from evolutionary psychology, epigenetics, paleoanthropology, and neuroscience, we examine whether tens of thousands of years of competition, conflict, and potentially traumatic interactions between human species could have left an indelible mark on our collective psychology. While speculative, this hypothesis offers a compelling framework for understanding one of psychology's most intriguing phenomena.

Introduction

The uncanny valley effect, first described by Japanese roboticist Masahiro Mori in 1970, represents one of the most fascinating puzzles in human psychology. This phenomenon describes the sharp decline in emotional response that occurs when artificial entities approach—but do not quite achieve—human likeness. As robots, animations, or mannequins become increasingly humanlike, people tend to respond with increasing empathy until a critical threshold is reached, at which point the response suddenly becomes one of profound unease, revulsion, or even fear.

While numerous theories have attempted to explain this phenomenon through cognitive and evolutionary frameworks, one intriguing possibility remains largely unexplored: that the uncanny valley represents an ancient survival mechanism, forged during the tens of thousands of years when our ancestors shared the planet with other human species—most notably, the Neanderthals.

This report examines the evidence supporting what we term the "Ancestral Fear Hypothesis"—the proposition that modern humans may carry inherited psychological responses to almost-human entities that originated from encounters with Neanderthals during the Upper Paleolithic period, approximately 40,000-100,000 years ago.

The Uncanny Valley: Current Understanding

DEFINING THE PHENOMENON

The uncanny valley hypothesis predicts that an entity appearing almost human will elicit feelings of eeriness, discomfort, or even revulsion in observers. This effect has been documented across diverse contexts, including humanoid robots, computer-generated imagery, lifelike dolls, animatronics, and prosthetic limbs. The phenomenon appears to be universal across cultures, suggesting a deep biological rather than purely cultural origin.

EXISTING THEORETICAL EXPLANATIONS

Current scientific literature proposes several mechanisms that may underlie the uncanny valley effect:

Mate Selection Theory: This explanation suggests that uncanny stimuli trigger evolved cognitive mechanisms for avoiding mates with signs of poor health, low fertility, or compromised immune function. Visible anomalies in almost-human faces may activate ancient warning systems designed to identify unsuitable reproductive partners.

Mortality Salience: The uncanny valley may activate unconscious fears about death and bodily integrity. Humanoid figures that appear "not quite alive" may remind us of corpses or the fragility of human existence, triggering existential anxiety and defensive responses.

Pathogen Avoidance: Perhaps most relevant to our hypothesis, this theory proposes that the uncanny valley activates disease-avoidance mechanisms. Visual anomalies in human-like entities may be processed as indicators of infection, parasitism, or contagion. Notably, research suggests that "the more human an organism looks, the stronger the aversion to its defects, because defects indicate disease, more human-looking organisms are more closely related to human beings genetically, and the probability of contracting disease-causing bacteria, viruses, and other parasites increases with genetic similarity."

Violation of Human Norms: When an entity appears almost human, it activates our cognitive models for normal human beings, causing nonhuman characteristics to become jarring and disturbing. The brain expects a human but detects subtle wrongness.

Conflicting Perceptual Cues: The discomfort may arise from cognitive conflict when processing entities that provide mixed signals about their category membership—neither clearly human nor clearly nonhuman.

The Neanderthal Context: A Shared World

COEXISTENCE AND CONTACT

For tens of thousands of years, Homo sapiens and Neanderthals shared overlapping territories across Europe and western Asia. Archaeological and genetic evidence indicates prolonged periods of contact between these two human species, with interactions ranging from peaceful coexistence and interbreeding to competition and potentially violent conflict.

DNA evidence indicates that Homo sapiens had contact with Neanderthals and genetic admixture as early as 120,000-100,000 years ago. The extinction of Neanderthals occurred approximately 40,000 years ago, meaning our ancestors coexisted with this other human species for at least 60,000-80,000 years—more than enough time for significant psychological adaptations to develop.

THE NEANDERTHAL APPEARANCE

Neanderthals would have presented a profoundly uncanny sight to early modern humans. While clearly humanlike in overall form and behavior, they possessed distinctive physical features that would have set them apart:

- Larger, more robust build with barrel-shaped chests
- Distinctive facial features including pronounced brow ridges
- Larger noses adapted for cold climates
- Different cranial shape with a more elongated skull
- Slightly different proportions in limbs and body

Importantly, Neanderthals were close enough to Homo sapiens to interbreed successfully, yet different enough to be immediately recognizable as "other." This combination—human enough to be familiar, yet different enough to be unsettling—mirrors precisely the conditions that trigger the uncanny valley response today.

EVIDENCE OF CONFLICT AND VIOLENCE

The hypothesis that early humans violently replaced Neanderthals was first proposed by French paleontologist Marcellin Boule in 1912. Modern research supports the likelihood of violent encounters between species. Researcher Kwang Hyun Ko has documented evidence suggesting that Neanderthal extinction was either precipitated or hastened by violent conflict with Homo sapiens.

Violence in early hunter-gatherer societies typically occurred as a result of resource competition, particularly following environmental changes or natural disasters. Given that both species competed for similar resources in overlapping territories, violent encounters would have been virtually inevitable over tens of thousands of years of coexistence.

CANNIBALISM EVIDENCE

Archaeological evidence from multiple sites demonstrates that Neanderthals practiced cannibalism to some extent. Sites such as Cueva del Sidrón in Spain have yielded Neanderthal remains showing clear evidence of butchering marks consistent with defleshing and marrow extraction. Whether this cannibalism was ritualistic, survival-driven, or predatory remains debated, but the evidence is clear that Neanderthals consumed other Neanderthals.

More provocatively, some researchers have speculated about inter-species consumption. The discovery of the PRNP gene 129 variant—which provides immunity to prion diseases transmitted through cannibalism—is widespread among all modern humans. British palaeoanthropologist Simon Underdown has speculated that this genetic signature might indicate that cannibalistic practices involving both species may have occurred during the period of coexistence.

Transgenerational Trauma & Epigenetic Inheritance

THE SCIENCE OF INHERITED FEAR

One of the most crucial pillars supporting the Ancestral Fear Hypothesis is the emerging science of transgenerational trauma and epigenetic inheritance. Research has demonstrated that traumatic experiences can leave biological marks that persist across generations, potentially allowing survival-relevant information to be passed from parents to offspring.

THE DIAS AND RESSLER STUDY

The groundbreaking 2013 study by Brian Dias and Kerry Ressler at Emory University provided compelling evidence that fear responses can be inherited across generations. In this landmark research, mice were conditioned to fear a specific odor (acetophenone, which smells like cherry blossoms) by pairing exposure to the scent with mild foot shocks.

Remarkably, the offspring of these conditioned mice—conceived after the fear conditioning and raised by unconditioned parents—showed heightened sensitivity and fear responses to the same odor, despite never having been exposed to it before. This enhanced sensitivity persisted into the third generation (F2), demonstrating true transgenerational inheritance.

The study revealed several key findings:

- F1 and F2 generations showed increased behavioral sensitivity to the conditioned odor but not to other odors
- Enhanced neuroanatomical representation of the relevant olfactory pathway was observed
- Bisulfite sequencing revealed CpG hypomethylation in the relevant odorant receptor gene in sperm DNA
- Cross-fostering and in vitro fertilization experiments confirmed that effects were inherited via gametes, not learned behavior

This research provides a mechanism by which traumatic encounters with Neanderthals could have left lasting marks on the human genome, potentially encoding fear responses to "almost-human" entities that persist to the present day.

MECHANISMS OF TRANSMISSION

Transgenerational trauma can be transmitted through several pathways:

Epigenetic Modifications: Changes in gene expression that do not alter the underlying DNA sequence but can be passed to offspring. These include DNA methylation patterns and histone modifications that affect how genes are read and expressed.

Germline Transmission: Direct transmission through sperm or egg cells, as demonstrated in the Dias and Ressler study. This represents true biological inheritance of acquired characteristics.

Developmental Programming: Stress hormones and other factors during pregnancy can affect fetal development, potentially programming offspring for heightened threat sensitivity.

While the hypothesis of epigenetic inheritance of trauma in humans remains controversial and requires further research, the animal studies provide proof-of-concept that such transmission is biologically possible.

The Ancestral Fear Hypothesis: Synthesis

THE PROPOSED MECHANISM

We propose that the uncanny valley response represents an inherited fear response that developed during the prolonged period of Homo sapiens-Neanderthal coexistence. The mechanism would have operated as follows:

1. Initial Trauma: Early modern humans encountered Neanderthals as competitors for resources, potential predators or prey in cannibalistic encounters, and sources of novel diseases. These encounters were likely traumatic and frequently fatal.

2. Adaptive Fear Response: Individuals who developed automatic fear and avoidance responses to Neanderthal-like features—entities that appeared almost human but subtly wrong—gained survival advantages. This would have facilitated quick identification of threats and appropriate defensive responses.
3. Epigenetic Encoding: Through mechanisms similar to those demonstrated in the Dias and Ressler study, these fear responses became encoded in epigenetic modifications that could be passed to offspring.
4. Selection Pressure: Over tens of thousands of years, selection pressure would have favored individuals carrying these inherited fear responses, as they would be more likely to survive encounters with Neanderthals and other potentially dangerous hominins.
5. Persistence After Extinction: After Neanderthal extinction approximately 40,000 years ago, the inherited fear response remained, no longer serving its original adaptive purpose but still triggered by stimuli resembling the original threat—entities that appear almost human but not quite right.

SUPPORTING EVIDENCE

Several lines of evidence support this hypothesis:

Universality: The uncanny valley effect appears across all human cultures, suggesting a biological rather than cultural origin. An inherited fear response would explain this cross-cultural consistency.

Automatic Response: The uncanny valley response is largely automatic and unconscious, consistent with an evolved fear mechanism rather than a learned response. Research shows that even infants display discomfort with uncanny stimuli.

Specificity to Human Likeness: The effect specifically targets entities that approach human likeness—precisely what would be expected from a response evolved to detect Neanderthals and other hominins.

Connection to Disease Avoidance: The pathogen avoidance explanation for the uncanny valley aligns perfectly with the known disease transmission risks between closely related species. Modern humans may have carried diseases deadly to Neanderthals, and vice versa.

Genetic Evidence of Interbreeding: The presence of Neanderthal DNA in modern non-African populations (typically 1-4%) demonstrates intimate contact between species. This interbreeding would have created additional psychological complexity, as Neanderthals were simultaneously potential mates and potential threats.

Related Phenomena: Coulrophobia & Automatonophobia

FEAR OF CLOWNS

Coulrophobia—the irrational fear of clowns—affects a surprisingly large percentage of the population. A 2022 survey of 987 adults from 64 countries found that 54% of respondents reported experiencing some degree of coulrophobia.

Researchers have noted direct connections between coulrophobia and the uncanny valley effect. Clowns present a human face altered in specific ways—exaggerated features, hidden expressions, painted masks over human skin. As one psychology professor noted, young children are "very reactive to a familiar body type with an unfamiliar face."

Cultural critic Mark Dery has observed that clowns' makeup "hiding their faces, making them potential threats in disguise" may activate ancient threat detection systems. The chalk-white face in which "the eyes almost disappear, while the mouth is enlarged to a ghoulish bigness, looks like the mask of death."

Through the lens of the Ancestral Fear Hypothesis, coulrophobia may represent activation of the same ancient fear circuits—the clown's altered human face may trigger responses originally calibrated to detect Neanderthals or other dangerous hominins.

FEAR OF HUMAN-LIKE FIGURES

Automatonophobia—the fear of humanoid figures such as mannequins, wax figures, animatronics, and statues—represents another manifestation of uncanny valley-related fear. Sufferers report intense anxiety and even panic attacks when confronted with realistic human representations.

These phobias share key features with the proposed ancestral fear response: they are automatic, difficult to rationalize away, and specifically triggered by entities that approximate but do not quite achieve human likeness.

Implications and Future Research

TESTING THE HYPOTHESIS

While speculative, the Ancestral Fear Hypothesis generates several testable predictions:

1. Neuroimaging Studies: Brain imaging during uncanny valley exposure should reveal activation of ancient fear circuits, particularly the amygdala, rather than purely cognitive processing regions.
2. Cross-Cultural Research: Populations with different levels of Neanderthal admixture might show varying intensities of uncanny valley response, if the hypothesis is correct.
3. Developmental Studies: If the response is truly inherited rather than learned, it should ap-

pear very early in development, potentially even in infants.

4. Genetic Association Studies: Specific genetic variants related to fear processing might correlate with intensity of uncanny valley response.

BROADER IMPLICATIONS

The Ancestral Fear Hypothesis, if supported by further research, would have significant implications for multiple fields:

Robotics and AI: Understanding the biological basis of the uncanny valley could inform design strategies for humanoid robots and virtual agents, potentially allowing designers to avoid triggering ancestral fear responses.

Clinical Psychology: Phobias related to human-like figures might be understood as manifestations of inherited trauma, potentially informing treatment approaches.

Evolutionary Psychology: The hypothesis provides a concrete example of how ancestral encounters with other human species might have shaped modern psychological traits.

Paleoanthropology: Understanding psychological responses to Neanderthals might provide insight into the nature of interactions between species during the period of coexistence.

Limitations and Criticisms

SCIENTIFIC CAUTION

It is essential to acknowledge the speculative nature of this hypothesis and the limitations of current evidence:

Epigenetic Inheritance Controversy: While the Dias and Ressler study demonstrated epigenetic inheritance of fear in mice, the relevance to humans remains debated. Critics note that methylation is normally erased when an egg cell is fertilized, and conclusive evidence of epigenetic trauma inheritance in humans has not been established.

Alternative Explanations: The uncanny valley may be fully explained by existing theories such as pathogen avoidance, mortality salience, and perceptual conflict without requiring ancestral trauma.

Time Depth: Forty thousand years represents many thousands of generations. Whether epigenetic modifications could persist over such timescales is unknown.

Lack of Direct Evidence: We have no direct evidence of the psychological responses of ancient humans to Neanderthals.

Conclusion

The uncanny valley phenomenon remains one of psychology's most intriguing mysteries. While current explanations focus on cognitive and immediate evolutionary factors, the Ancestral Fear Hypothesis offers a deeper temporal perspective—one that connects our modern psychological responses to the ancient drama of human evolution.

For tens of thousands of years, our ancestors shared the world with other human species. These encounters—sometimes peaceful, sometimes violent, always consequential—shaped the trajectory of human evolution. It would be surprising if such profound experiences left no psychological trace.

Whether or not the uncanny valley ultimately proves to be an inherited response to Neanderthal encounters, the hypothesis illuminates important connections between our evolutionary past and present psychology. It reminds us that we are not merely products of our individual experiences but carry within us the accumulated wisdom—and perhaps the accumulated fears—of countless generations.

The visceral unease we feel when confronting an almost-human face may be more than a quirk of perception. It may be an echo from the deep past, a whispered warning from ancestors who learned, through terror and loss, to fear those who looked almost—but not quite—like us.

References

1. Mori, M. (1970). The Uncanny Valley. Energy, 7(4), 33-35.
2. Dias, B.G., & Ressler, K.J. (2014). Parental olfactory experience influences behavior and neural structure in subsequent generations. Nature Neuroscience, 17, 89-96.
3. Ko, K.H. (2016). Hominin interbreeding and the evolution of human variation. Journal of Biological Research, 23(1), 17.
4. Yehuda, R., & Lehrner, A. (2018). Intergenerational transmission of trauma effects: putative role of epigenetic mechanisms. World Psychiatry, 17(3), 243-257.
5. MacDorman, K.F., & Ishiguro, H. (2006). The uncanny advantage of using androids in cognitive and social science research. Interaction Studies, 7(3), 297-337.

6. Green, R.E., et al. (2010). A draft sequence of the Neandertal genome. Science, 328(5979), 710-722.
7. Underdown, S. (2008). A potential role for transmissible spongiform encephalopathies in Neanderthal extinction. Medical Hypotheses, 71(1), 4-7.
8. Mathur, M.B., & Reichling, D.B. (2016). Navigating a social world with robot partners: A quantitative cartography of the Uncanny Valley. Cognition, 146, 22-32.
9. Finlayson, C. (2004). Neanderthals and Modern Humans: An Ecological and Evolutionary Perspective. Cambridge University Press.
10. Radford, B. (2016). Bad Clowns. University of New Mexico Press.
11. Dery, M. (1999). The Pyrotechnic Insanitarium: American Culture on the Brink. Grove Press.
12. Prüfer, K., et al. (2014). The complete genome sequence of a Neanderthal from the Altai Mountains. Nature, 505(7481), 43-49.

www.ingramcontent.com/pod-product-compliance
Lightning Source LLC
LaVergne TN
LVHW022033200926
848481LV00007B/2666
* 9 7 9 8 2 9 5 4 8 2 0 7 6 *